My
Song Chord & Project
Notebook

By J.J. Allen

This Book Is The Property Of:

_____

IF Lost, Please Return To:

Address: _____
_____
_____
_____

For the Uninitiated,

Let's take some notes about your favorite musical combinations ... or just those worth remembering.

Regards,
J.J. Allen

Dedicated to the gifted and creative "Genius" inside of all of us that just can't remember everything.

A

Song: _____

Source:_____ Date: _____

Genre/Mood: _____ Tempo:_____

Chords/Notes:_____

_____

_____

_____

Song: _____

Source:_____ Date: _____

Genre/Mood: _____ Tempo:_____

Chords/Notes:_____

_____

_____

_____

Song: _____

Source:_____ Date: _____

Genre/Mood: _____ Tempo:_____

Chords/Notes:_____

_____

_____

_____

A

Song: _____

Source:_____ Date: _____

Genre/Mood: _____ Tempo: _____

Chords/Notes:_____

_____

_____

_____

Song: _____

Source:_____ Date: _____

Genre/Mood: _____ Tempo:_____

Chords/Notes:_____

_____

_____

_____

Song: _____

Source:_____ Date: _____

Genre/Mood: _____ Tempo:_____

Chords/Notes:_____

_____

_____

_____

Song: _____

Source:_____ Date: _____

Genre/Mood: _____ Tempo:_____

Chords/Notes:_____

_____

_____

_____

Song: _____

Source:_____ Date: _____

Genre/Mood: _____ Tempo:_____

Chords/Notes:_____

_____

_____

_____

Song: _____

Source:_____ Date: _____

Genre/Mood: _____ Tempo:_____

Chords/Notes:_____

_____

_____

_____

A

Song: _____

Source:_____ Date: _____

Genre/Mood: _____ Tempo: _____

Chords/Notes:_____

_____

_____

_____

Song: _____

Source:_____ Date: _____

Genre/Mood: _____ Tempo:_____

Chords/Notes:_____

_____

_____

_____

Song: _____

Source:_____ Date: _____

Genre/Mood: _____ Tempo:_____

Chords/Notes:_____

_____

_____

_____

Song: _____

Source:_____ Date: _____

Genre/Mood: _____ Tempo:_____

Chords/Notes:_____

_____

_____

_____

Song: _____

Source:_____ Date: _____

Genre/Mood: _____ Tempo:_____

Chords/Notes:_____

_____

_____

_____

Song: _____

Source:_____ Date: _____

Genre/Mood: _____ Tempo:_____

Chords/Notes:_____

_____

_____

_____

A

Song: _____

Source:_____ Date: _____

Genre/Mood: _____ Tempo: _____

Chords/Notes:_____

_____

_____

_____

Song: _____

Source:_____ Date: _____

Genre/Mood: _____ Tempo:_____

Chords/Notes:_____

_____

_____

_____

Song: _____

Source:_____ Date: _____

Genre/Mood: _____ Tempo:_____

Chords/Notes:_____

_____

_____

_____

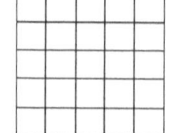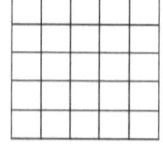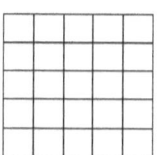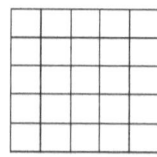

Song: _____

Source: _____ Date: _____

Genre/Mood: _____ Tempo: _____

Chords/Notes: _____

_____

_____

_____

B

Song: _____

Source: _____ Date: _____

Genre/Mood: _____ Tempo: _____

Chords/Notes: _____

_____

_____

_____

Song: _____

Source: _____ Date: _____

Genre/Mood: _____ Tempo: _____

Chords/Notes: _____

_____

_____

_____

Song: _____

Source:_____ Date: _____

Genre/Mood: _____ Tempo:_____

Chords/Notes:_____

_____

_____

_____

B

Song: _____

Source:_____ Date: _____

Genre/Mood: _____ Tempo:_____

Chords/Notes:_____

_____

_____

_____

Song: _____

Source:_____ Date: _____

Genre/Mood: _____ Tempo:_____

Chords/Notes:_____

_____

_____

_____

Song: _____

Source:_____ Date: _____

Genre/Mood: _____ Tempo:_____

Chords/Notes:_____

_____

_____

_____

Song: _____

Source:_____ Date: _____

Genre/Mood: _____ Tempo:_____

Chords/Notes:_____

_____

_____

_____

Song: _____

Source:_____ Date: _____

Genre/Mood: _____ Tempo:_____

Chords/Notes:_____

_____

_____

_____

Song: _____

Source:_____ Date: _____

Genre/Mood: _____ Tempo:_____

Chords/Notes:_____

_____

_____

_____

B

Song: _____

Source:_____ Date: _____

Genre/Mood: _____ Tempo:_____

Chords/Notes:_____

_____

_____

_____

Song: _____

Source:_____ Date: _____

Genre/Mood: _____ Tempo:_____

Chords/Notes:_____

_____

_____

_____

Song: _____

Source:_____ Date: _____

Genre/Mood: _____ Tempo:_____

Chords/Notes:_____

_____

_____

_____

Song: _____

Source:_____ Date: _____

Genre/Mood: _____ Tempo:_____

Chords/Notes:_____

_____

_____

_____

Song: _____

Source:_____ Date: _____

Genre/Mood: _____ Tempo:_____

Chords/Notes:_____

_____

_____

_____

Song: _____

Source:_____ Date: _____

Genre/Mood: _____ Tempo:_____

Chords/Notes:_____

_____

_____

_____

B

Song: _____

Source:_____ Date: _____

Genre/Mood: _____ Tempo:_____

Chords/Notes:_____

_____

_____

_____

Song: _____

Source:_____ Date: _____

Genre/Mood: _____ Tempo:_____

Chords/Notes:_____

_____

_____

_____

Song: _____

Source:_____ Date: _____

Genre/Mood: _____ Tempo:_____

Chords/Notes:_____

_____

_____

_____

Song: _____

Source:_____ Date: _____

Genre/Mood: _____ Tempo:_____

Chords/Notes:_____

_____

_____

_____

C

Song: _____

Source:_____ Date: _____

Genre/Mood: _____ Tempo:_____

Chords/Notes:_____

_____

_____

_____

Song: _____

Source:_____ Date: _____

Genre/Mood: _____ Tempo:_____

Chords/Notes:_____

_____

_____

_____

Song: _____

Source:_____ Date: _____

Genre/Mood: _____ Tempo:_____

Chords/Notes:_____

_____

_____

_____

C

Song: _____

Source:_____ Date: _____

Genre/Mood: _____ Tempo:_____

Chords/Notes:_____

_____

_____

_____

Song: _____

Source:_____ Date: _____

Genre/Mood: _____ Tempo:_____

Chords/Notes:_____

_____

_____

_____

Song: _____

Source:_____ Date: _____

Genre/Mood: _____ Tempo:_____

Chords/Notes:_____

_____

_____

_____

C

Song: _____

Source:_____ Date: _____

Genre/Mood: _____ Tempo:_____

Chords/Notes:_____

_____

_____

_____

Song: _____

Source:_____ Date: _____

Genre/Mood: _____ Tempo:_____

Chords/Notes:_____

_____

_____

_____

Song: _____

Source:_____ Date: _____

Genre/Mood: _____ Tempo:_____

Chords/Notes:_____

_____

_____

_____

C

Song: _____

Source:_____ Date: _____

Genre/Mood: _____ Tempo:_____

Chords/Notes:_____

_____

_____

_____

Song: _____

Source:_____ Date: _____

Genre/Mood: _____ Tempo:_____

Chords/Notes:_____

_____

_____

_____

Song: _____

Source:_____ Date: _____

Genre/Mood: _____ Tempo:_____

Chords/Notes:_____

_____

_____

_____

C

Song: _____

Source:_____ Date: _____

Genre/Mood: _____ Tempo:_____

Chords/Notes:_____

_____

_____

_____

Song: _____

Source:_____ Date: _____

Genre/Mood: _____ Tempo:_____

Chords/Notes:_____

_____

_____

_____

Song: _____

Source:_____ Date: _____

Genre/Mood: _____ Tempo:_____

Chords/Notes:_____

_____

_____

_____

C

Song: _____

Source:_____ Date: _____

Genre/Mood: _____ Tempo:_____

Chords/Notes:_____

_____

_____

_____

Song: _____

Source:_____ Date: _____

Genre/Mood: _____ Tempo:_____

Chords/Notes:_____

_____

_____

_____

Song: _____

Source:_____ Date: _____

Genre/Mood: _____ Tempo:_____

Chords/Notes:_____

_____

_____

_____

Song: _____

Source:_____ Date: _____

Genre/Mood: _____ Tempo:_____

Chords/Notes:_____

_____

_____

_____

D

Song: _____

Source:_____ Date: _____

Genre/Mood: _____ Tempo:_____

Chords/Notes:_____

_____

_____

_____

Song: _____

Source:_____ Date: _____

Genre/Mood: _____ Tempo:_____

Chords/Notes:_____

_____

_____

_____

Song: _____

Source:_____ Date: _____

Genre/Mood: _____ Tempo:_____

Chords/Notes:_____

_____

_____

_____

D

Song: _____

Source:_____ Date: _____

Genre/Mood: _____ Tempo:_____

Chords/Notes:_____

_____

_____

_____

Song: _____

Source:_____ Date: _____

Genre/Mood: _____ Tempo:_____

Chords/Notes:_____

_____

_____

_____

Song: _____

Source:_____ Date: _____

Genre/Mood: _____ Tempo:_____

Chords/Notes:_____

_____

_____

_____

D

Song: _____

Source:_____ Date: _____

Genre/Mood: _____ Tempo:_____

Chords/Notes:_____

_____

_____

_____

Song: _____

Source:_____ Date: _____

Genre/Mood: _____ Tempo:_____

Chords/Notes:_____

_____

_____

_____

Song: _____

Source:_____ Date: _____

Genre/Mood: _____ Tempo:_____

Chords/Notes:_____

_____

_____

_____

D

Song: _____

Source:_____ Date: _____

Genre/Mood: _____ Tempo:_____

Chords/Notes:_____

_____

_____

_____

Song: _____

Source:_____ Date: _____

Genre/Mood: _____ Tempo:_____

Chords/Notes:_____

_____

_____

_____

Song: _____

Source:_____ Date: _____

Genre/Mood: _____ Tempo:_____

Chords/Notes:_____

_____

_____

_____

D

Song: _____

Source:_____ Date: _____

Genre/Mood: _____ Tempo:_____

Chords/Notes:_____

_____

_____

_____

Song: _____

Source:_____ Date: _____

Genre/Mood: _____ Tempo:_____

Chords/Notes:_____

_____

_____

_____

Song: _____

Source:_____ Date: _____

Genre/Mood: _____ Tempo:_____

Chords/Notes:_____

_____

_____

_____

D

Song: _____

Source:_____ Date: _____

Genre/Mood: _____ Tempo:_____

Chords/Notes:_____

_____

_____

_____

Song: _____

Source:_____ Date: _____

Genre/Mood: _____ Tempo:_____

Chords/Notes:_____

_____

_____

_____

Song: _____

Source:_____ Date: _____

Genre/Mood: _____ Tempo:_____

Chords/Notes:_____

_____

_____

_____

E

Song: _____

Source:_____ Date: _____

Genre/Mood: _____ Tempo: _____

Chords/Notes: _____

_____

_____

_____

Song: _____

Source:_____ Date: _____

Genre/Mood: _____ Tempo:_____

Chords/Notes:_____

_____

_____

_____

Song: _____

Source:_____ Date: _____

Genre/Mood: _____ Tempo:_____

Chords/Notes:_____

_____

_____

_____

Song: _____

Source:_____ Date: _____

Genre/Mood: _____ Tempo:_____

Chords/Notes:_____

_____

_____

_____

Song: _____

Source:_____ Date: _____

Genre/Mood: _____ Tempo:_____

Chords/Notes:_____

_____

_____

_____

Song: _____

Source:_____ Date: _____

Genre/Mood: _____ Tempo:_____

Chords/Notes:_____

_____

_____

_____

E

Song: _____

Source:_____ Date: _____

Genre/Mood: _____ Tempo: _____

Chords/Notes: _____

_____

_____

_____

Song: _____

Source:_____ Date: _____

Genre/Mood: _____ Tempo:_____

Chords/Notes:_____

_____

_____

_____

Song: _____

Source:_____ Date: _____

Genre/Mood: _____ Tempo:_____

Chords/Notes:_____

_____

_____

_____

Song: _____

Source:_____ Date: _____

Genre/Mood: _____ Tempo:_____

Chords/Notes:_____

_____

_____

_____

Song: _____

Source:_____ Date: _____

Genre/Mood: _____ Tempo:_____

Chords/Notes:_____

_____

_____

_____

Song: _____

Source:_____ Date: _____

Genre/Mood: _____ Tempo:_____

Chords/Notes:_____

_____

_____

_____

E

Song: _____

Source: _____ Date: _____

Genre/Mood: _____ Tempo: _____

Chords/Notes: _____

_____

_____

_____

Song: _____

Source: _____ Date: _____

Genre/Mood: _____ Tempo: _____

Chords/Notes: _____

_____

_____

_____

Song: _____

Source: _____ Date: _____

Genre/Mood: _____ Tempo: _____

Chords/Notes: _____

_____

_____

_____

Song: _____

Source:_____ Date: _____

Genre/Mood: _____ Tempo:_____

Chords/Notes:_____

_____

_____

_____

F

Song: _____

Source:_____ Date: _____

Genre/Mood: _____ Tempo:_____

Chords/Notes:_____

_____

_____

_____

Song: _____

Source:_____ Date: _____

Genre/Mood: _____ Tempo:_____

Chords/Notes:_____

_____

_____

_____

Song: _____

Source:_____ Date: _____

Genre/Mood: _____ Tempo:_____

Chords/Notes:_____

_____

_____

_____

F

Song: _____

Source:_____ Date: _____

Genre/Mood: _____ Tempo:_____

Chords/Notes:_____

_____

_____

_____

Song: _____

Source:_____ Date: _____

Genre/Mood: _____ Tempo:_____

Chords/Notes:_____

_____

_____

_____

Song: _____

Source:_____ Date: _____

Genre/Mood: _____ Tempo:_____

Chords/Notes:_____

_____

_____

_____

F

Song: _____

Source:_____ Date: _____

Genre/Mood: _____ Tempo:_____

Chords/Notes:_____

_____

_____

_____

Song: _____

Source:_____ Date: _____

Genre/Mood: _____ Tempo:_____

Chords/Notes:_____

_____

_____

_____

Song: _____

Source:_____ Date: _____

Genre/Mood: _____ Tempo:_____

Chords/Notes:_____

_____

_____

_____

F

Song: _____

Source:_____ Date: _____

Genre/Mood: _____ Tempo:_____

Chords/Notes:_____

_____

_____

_____

Song: _____

Source:_____ Date: _____

Genre/Mood: _____ Tempo:_____

Chords/Notes:_____

_____

_____

_____

Song: _____

Source:_____ Date: _____

Genre/Mood: _____ Tempo:_____

Chords/Notes:_____

_____

_____

_____

F

Song: _____

Source:_____ Date: _____

Genre/Mood: _____ Tempo:_____

Chords/Notes:_____

_____

_____

_____

Song: _____

Source:_____ Date: _____

Genre/Mood: _____ Tempo:_____

Chords/Notes:_____

_____

_____

_____

Song: _____

Source:_____ Date: _____

Genre/Mood: _____ Tempo:_____

Chords/Notes:_____

_____

_____

_____

F

Song: _____

Source:_____ Date: _____

Genre/Mood: _____ Tempo:_____

Chords/Notes:_____

_____

_____

_____

Song: _____

Source:_____ Date: _____

Genre/Mood: _____ Tempo:_____

Chords/Notes:_____

_____

_____

_____

Song: _____

Source:_____ Date: _____

Genre/Mood: _____ Tempo:_____

Chords/Notes:_____

_____

_____

_____

Song: _____

Source:_____ Date: _____

Genre/Mood: _____ Tempo:_____

Chords/Notes:_____

_____

_____

_____

Song: _____

Source:_____ Date: _____

Genre/Mood: _____ Tempo:_____

Chords/Notes:_____

_____

_____

_____

Song: _____

Source:_____ Date: _____

Genre/Mood: _____ Tempo:_____

Chords/Notes:_____

_____

_____

_____

Song: _____

Source:_____ Date: _____

Genre/Mood: _____ Tempo:_____

Chords/Notes:_____

_____

_____

_____

G

Song: _____

Source:_____ Date: _____

Genre/Mood: _____ Tempo:_____

Chords/Notes:_____

_____

_____

_____

Song: _____

Source:_____ Date: _____

Genre/Mood: _____ Tempo:_____

Chords/Notes:_____

_____

_____

_____

Song: _____

Source:_____ Date: _____

Genre/Mood: _____ Tempo:_____

Chords/Notes:_____

_____

_____

_____

G

Song: _____

Source:_____ Date: _____

Genre/Mood: _____ Tempo:_____

Chords/Notes:_____

_____

_____

_____

Song: _____

Source:_____ Date: _____

Genre/Mood: _____ Tempo:_____

Chords/Notes:_____

_____

_____

_____

Song: _____

Source:_____ Date: _____

Genre/Mood: _____ Tempo:_____

Chords/Notes:_____

_____

_____

_____

G

Song: _____

Source:_____ Date: _____

Genre/Mood: _____ Tempo:_____

Chords/Notes:_____

_____

_____

_____

Song: _____

Source:_____ Date: _____

Genre/Mood: _____ Tempo:_____

Chords/Notes:_____

_____

_____

_____

Song: _____

Source:_____ Date: _____

Genre/Mood: _____ Tempo:_____

Chords/Notes:_____

_____

_____

_____

G

Song: _____

Source:_____ Date: _____

Genre/Mood: _____ Tempo:_____

Chords/Notes:_____

_____

_____

_____

Song: _____

Source:_____ Date: _____

Genre/Mood: _____ Tempo:_____

Chords/Notes:_____

_____

_____

_____

Song: _____

Source:_____ Date: _____

Genre/Mood: _____ Tempo:_____

Chords/Notes:_____

_____

_____

_____

G

Song: _____

Source:_____ Date: _____

Genre/Mood: _____ Tempo:_____

Chords/Notes:_____

_____

_____

_____

Song: _____

Source:_____ Date: _____

Genre/Mood: _____ Tempo:_____

Chords/Notes:_____

_____

_____

_____

Song: _____

Source:_____ Date: _____

Genre/Mood: _____ Tempo:_____

Chords/Notes:_____

_____

_____

_____

Song: _____

Source:_____ Date: _____

Genre/Mood: _____ Tempo:_____

Chords/Notes:_____

_____

_____

_____

H

Song: _____

Source:_____ Date: _____

Genre/Mood: _____ Tempo:_____

Chords/Notes:_____

_____

_____

_____

Song: _____

Source:_____ Date: _____

Genre/Mood: _____ Tempo:_____

Chords/Notes:_____

_____

_____

_____

Song: _____

Source:_____ Date: _____

Genre/Mood: _____ Tempo:_____

Chords/Notes:_____

_____

_____

_____

H

Song: _____

Source:_____ Date: _____

Genre/Mood: _____ Tempo:_____

Chords/Notes:_____

_____

_____

_____

Song: _____

Source:_____ Date: _____

Genre/Mood: _____ Tempo:_____

Chords/Notes:_____

_____

_____

_____

Song: _____

Source:_____ Date: _____

Genre/Mood: _____ Tempo:_____

Chords/Notes:_____

_____

_____

_____

H

Song: _____

Source:_____ Date: _____

Genre/Mood: _____ Tempo:_____

Chords/Notes:_____

_____

_____

_____

Song: _____

Source:_____ Date: _____

Genre/Mood: _____ Tempo:_____

Chords/Notes:_____

_____

_____

_____

Song: _____

Source:_____ Date: _____

Genre/Mood: _____ Tempo:_____

Chords/Notes:_____

_____

_____

_____

H

Song: _____

Source:_____ Date: _____

Genre/Mood: _____ Tempo:_____

Chords/Notes:_____

_____

_____

_____

Song: _____

Source:_____ Date: _____

Genre/Mood: _____ Tempo:_____

Chords/Notes:_____

_____

_____

_____

Song: _____

Source:_____ Date: _____

Genre/Mood: _____ Tempo:_____

Chords/Notes:_____

_____

_____

_____

H

Song: _____

Source:_____ Date: _____

Genre/Mood: _____ Tempo:_____

Chords/Notes:_____

_____

_____

_____

Song: _____

Source:_____ Date: _____

Genre/Mood: _____ Tempo:_____

Chords/Notes:_____

_____

_____

_____

Song: _____

Source:_____ Date: _____

Genre/Mood: _____ Tempo:_____

Chords/Notes:_____

_____

_____

_____

H

Song: _____

Source:_____ Date: _____

Genre/Mood: _____ Tempo:_____

Chords/Notes:_____

_____

_____

_____

Song: _____

Source:_____ Date: _____

Genre/Mood: _____ Tempo:_____

Chords/Notes:_____

_____

_____

_____

Song: _____

Source:_____ Date: _____

Genre/Mood: _____ Tempo:_____

Chords/Notes:_____

_____

_____

_____

I

Song: _____
Source:_____ Date: _____
Genre/Mood: _____ Tempo: _____
Chords/Notes: _____

_____
_____
_____

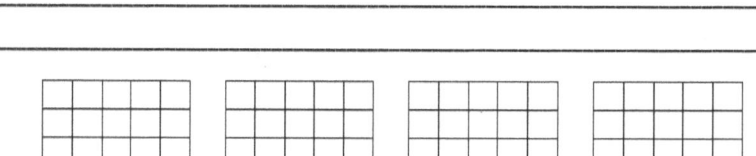

Song: _____
Source:_____ Date: _____
Genre/Mood: _____ Tempo:_____
Chords/Notes:_____

_____
_____
_____

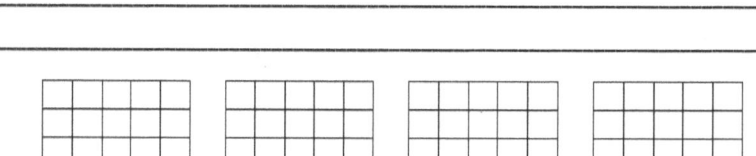

Song: _____
Source:_____ Date: _____
Genre/Mood: _____ Tempo:_____
Chords/Notes:_____

_____
_____
_____

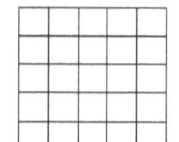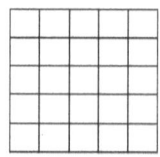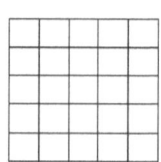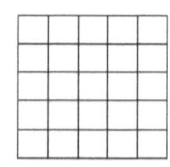

Song: _____

Source:_____ Date: _____

Genre/Mood: _____ Tempo:_____

Chords/Notes:_____

_____

_____

_____

Song: _____

Source:_____ Date: _____

Genre/Mood: _____ Tempo:_____

Chords/Notes:_____

_____

_____

_____

Song: _____

Source:_____ Date: _____

Genre/Mood: _____ Tempo:_____

Chords/Notes:_____

_____

_____

_____

Song: _____

Source:_____ Date: _____

Genre/Mood: _____ Tempo: _____

Chords/Notes: _____

_____

_____

_____

Song: _____

Source:_____ Date: _____

Genre/Mood: _____ Tempo:_____

Chords/Notes:_____

_____

_____

_____

Song: _____

Source:_____ Date: _____

Genre/Mood: _____ Tempo:_____

Chords/Notes:_____

_____

_____

_____

Song: _____

Source:_____ Date: _____

Genre/Mood: _____ Tempo:_____

Chords/Notes:_____

_____

_____

_____

Song: _____

Source:_____ Date: _____

Genre/Mood: _____ Tempo:_____

Chords/Notes:_____

_____

_____

_____

Song: _____

Source:_____ Date: _____

Genre/Mood: _____ Tempo:_____

Chords/Notes:_____

_____

_____

_____

I

Song: _____

Source:_____ Date: _____

Genre/Mood: _____ Tempo: _____

Chords/Notes: _____

_____

_____

_____

Song: _____

Source:_____ Date: _____

Genre/Mood: _____ Tempo:_____

Chords/Notes:_____

_____

_____

_____

Song: _____

Source:_____ Date: _____

Genre/Mood: _____ Tempo:_____

Chords/Notes:_____

_____

_____

_____

Song: _____

Source:_____ Date: _____

Genre/Mood: _____ Tempo:_____

Chords/Notes:_____

_____

_____

_____

J

Song: _____

Source:_____ Date: _____

Genre/Mood: _____ Tempo:_____

Chords/Notes:_____

_____

_____

_____

Song: _____

Source:_____ Date: _____

Genre/Mood: _____ Tempo:_____

Chords/Notes:_____

_____

_____

_____

Song: _____

Source:_____ Date: _____

Genre/Mood: _____ Tempo:_____

Chords/Notes:_____

_____

_____

_____

J

Song: _____

Source:_____ Date: _____

Genre/Mood: _____ Tempo:_____

Chords/Notes:_____

_____

_____

_____

Song: _____

Source:_____ Date: _____

Genre/Mood: _____ Tempo:_____

Chords/Notes:_____

_____

_____

_____

Song: _____

Source:_____ Date: _____

Genre/Mood: _____ Tempo:_____

Chords/Notes:_____

_____

_____

_____

Song: _____

Source:_____ Date: _____

Genre/Mood: _____ Tempo:_____

Chords/Notes:_____

_____

_____

_____

Song: _____

Source:_____ Date: _____

Genre/Mood: _____ Tempo:_____

Chords/Notes:_____

_____

_____

_____

Song: _____

Source:_____ Date: _____

Genre/Mood: _____ Tempo:_____

Chords/Notes:_____

_____

_____

_____

J

Song: _____

Source:_____ Date: _____

Genre/Mood: _____ Tempo:_____

Chords/Notes:_____

_____

_____

_____

Song: _____

Source:_____ Date: _____

Genre/Mood: _____ Tempo:_____

Chords/Notes:_____

_____

_____

_____

Song: _____

Source:_____ Date: _____

Genre/Mood: _____ Tempo:_____

Chords/Notes:_____

_____

_____

_____

Song: _____

Source:_____ Date: _____

Genre/Mood: _____ Tempo:_____

Chords/Notes:_____

_____

_____

_____

Song: _____

Source:_____ Date: _____

Genre/Mood: _____ Tempo:_____

Chords/Notes:_____

_____

_____

_____

Song: _____

Source:_____ Date: _____

Genre/Mood: _____ Tempo:_____

Chords/Notes:_____

_____

_____

_____

Song: _____

Source:_____ Date: _____

Genre/Mood: _____ Tempo:_____

Chords/Notes:_____

_____

_____

_____

Song: _____

Source:_____ Date: _____

Genre/Mood: _____ Tempo:_____

Chords/Notes:_____

_____

_____

_____

Song: _____
Source:_____ Date: _____
Genre/Mood: _____ Tempo:_____
Chords/Notes:_____
_____
_____
_____

Song: _____
Source:_____ Date: _____
Genre/Mood: _____ Tempo:_____
Chords/Notes:_____
_____
_____
_____

K

Song: _____
Source:_____ Date: _____
Genre/Mood: _____ Tempo:_____
Chords/Notes:_____
_____
_____
_____

Song: _____

Source:_____ Date: _____

Genre/Mood: _____ Tempo:_____

Chords/Notes:_____

_____

_____

_____

Song: _____

Source:_____ Date: _____

Genre/Mood: _____ Tempo:_____

Chords/Notes:_____

_____

_____

_____

K

Song: _____

Source:_____ Date: _____

Genre/Mood: _____ Tempo:_____

Chords/Notes:_____

_____

_____

_____

Song: _____

Source:_____ Date: _____

Genre/Mood: _____ Tempo:_____

Chords/Notes:_____

_____

_____

_____

Song: _____

Source:_____ Date: _____

Genre/Mood: _____ Tempo:_____

Chords/Notes:_____

_____

_____

_____

Song: _____

Source:_____ Date: _____

Genre/Mood: _____ Tempo:_____

Chords/Notes:_____

_____

_____

_____

Song: _____

Source:_____ Date: _____

Genre/Mood: _____ Tempo:_____

Chords/Notes:_____

_____

_____

_____

Song: _____

Source:_____ Date: _____

Genre/Mood: _____ Tempo:_____

Chords/Notes:_____

_____

_____

_____

K

Song: _____

Source:_____ Date: _____

Genre/Mood: _____ Tempo:_____

Chords/Notes:_____

_____

_____

_____

Song: _____

Source:_____ Date: _____

Genre/Mood: _____ Tempo:_____

Chords/Notes:_____

_____

_____

_____

Song: _____

Source:_____ Date: _____

Genre/Mood: _____ Tempo:_____

Chords/Notes:_____

_____

_____

_____

Song: _____

Source:_____ Date: _____

Genre/Mood: _____ Tempo:_____

Chords/Notes:_____

_____

_____

_____

Song: _____

Source:_____ Date: _____

Genre/Mood: _____ Tempo:_____

Chords/Notes:_____

_____

_____

_____

Song: _____

Source:_____ Date: _____

Genre/Mood: _____ Tempo:_____

Chords/Notes:_____

_____

_____

_____

K

Song: _____

Source:_____ Date: _____

Genre/Mood: _____ Tempo:_____

Chords/Notes:_____

_____

_____

_____

Song: _____

Source:_____ Date: _____

Genre/Mood: _____ Tempo:_____

Chords/Notes:_____

_____

_____

_____

Song: _____

Source:_____ Date: _____

Genre/Mood: _____ Tempo:_____

Chords/Notes:_____

_____

_____

_____

Song: _____

Source:_____ Date: _____

Genre/Mood: _____ Tempo:_____

Chords/Notes:_____

_____

_____

_____

L

Song: _____

Source:_____ Date: _____

Genre/Mood: _____ Tempo:_____

Chords/Notes:_____

_____

_____

_____

Song: _____

Source:_____ Date: _____

Genre/Mood: _____ Tempo:_____

Chords/Notes:_____

_____

_____

_____

Song: _____

Source:_____ Date: _____

Genre/Mood: _____ Tempo:_____

Chords/Notes:_____

_____

_____

_____

L

Song: _____

Source:_____ Date: _____

Genre/Mood: _____ Tempo:_____

Chords/Notes:_____

_____

_____

_____

Song: _____

Source:_____ Date: _____

Genre/Mood: _____ Tempo:_____

Chords/Notes:_____

_____

_____

_____

Song: _____

Source:_____ Date: _____

Genre/Mood: _____ Tempo:_____

Chords/Notes:_____

_____

_____

_____

L

Song: _____

Source:_____ Date: _____

Genre/Mood: _____ Tempo:_____

Chords/Notes:_____

_____

_____

_____

Song: _____

Source:_____ Date: _____

Genre/Mood: _____ Tempo:_____

Chords/Notes:_____

_____

_____

_____

Song: _____

Source:_____ Date: _____

Genre/Mood: _____ Tempo:_____

Chords/Notes:_____

_____

_____

_____

L

Song: _____

Source:_____ Date: _____

Genre/Mood: _____ Tempo:_____

Chords/Notes:_____

_____

_____

_____

Song: _____

Source:_____ Date: _____

Genre/Mood: _____ Tempo:_____

Chords/Notes:_____

_____

_____

_____

Song: _____

Source:_____ Date: _____

Genre/Mood: _____ Tempo:_____

Chords/Notes:_____

_____

_____

_____

L

Song: _____

Source:_____ Date: _____

Genre/Mood: _____ Tempo:_____

Chords/Notes:_____

_____

_____

_____

Song: _____

Source:_____ Date: _____

Genre/Mood: _____ Tempo:_____

Chords/Notes:_____

_____

_____

_____

Song: _____

Source:_____ Date: _____

Genre/Mood: _____ Tempo:_____

Chords/Notes:_____

_____

_____

_____

L

Song: _____

Source:_____ Date: _____

Genre/Mood: _____ Tempo:_____

Chords/Notes:_____

_____

_____

_____

Song: _____

Source:_____ Date: _____

Genre/Mood: _____ Tempo:_____

Chords/Notes:_____

_____

_____

_____

Song: _____

Source:_____ Date: _____

Genre/Mood: _____ Tempo:_____

Chords/Notes:_____

_____

_____

_____

M

Song: _____

Source:_____ Date: _____

Genre/Mood: _____ Tempo: _____

Chords/Notes: _____

_____

_____

_____

Song: _____

Source:_____ Date: _____

Genre/Mood: _____ Tempo:_____

Chords/Notes:_____

_____

_____

_____

Song: _____

Source:_____ Date: _____

Genre/Mood: _____ Tempo:_____

Chords/Notes:_____

_____

_____

_____

Song: _____

Source:_____ Date: _____

Genre/Mood: _____ Tempo:_____

Chords/Notes:_____

_____

_____

_____

Song: _____

Source:_____ Date: _____

Genre/Mood: _____ Tempo:_____

Chords/Notes:_____

_____ ∕

_____

_____

Song: _____

Source:_____ Date: _____

Genre/Mood: _____ Tempo:_____

Chords/Notes:_____

_____

_____

_____

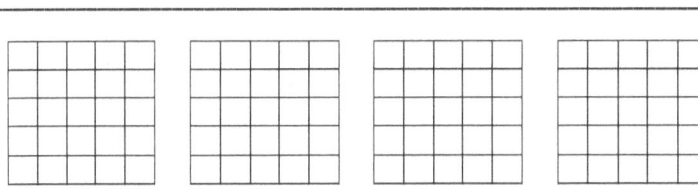

M

Song: _____

Source:_____ Date: _____

Genre/Mood: _____ Tempo: _____

Chords/Notes: _____

_____

_____

_____

Song: _____

Source:_____ Date: _____

Genre/Mood: _____ Tempo:_____

Chords/Notes:_____

_____

_____

_____

Song: _____

Source:_____ Date: _____

Genre/Mood: _____ Tempo:_____

Chords/Notes:_____

_____

_____

_____

Song: _____

Source:_____ Date: _____

Genre/Mood: _____ Tempo:_____

Chords/Notes:_____

_____

_____

_____

Song: _____

Source:_____ Date: _____

Genre/Mood: _____ Tempo:_____

Chords/Notes:_____

_____

_____

_____

Song: _____

Source:_____ Date: _____

Genre/Mood: _____ Tempo:_____

Chords/Notes:_____

_____

_____

_____

M

Song: _____

Source:_____ Date: _____

Genre/Mood: _____ Tempo: _____

Chords/Notes: _____

_____

_____

_____

Song: _____

Source:_____ Date: _____

Genre/Mood: _____ Tempo:_____

Chords/Notes:_____

_____

_____

_____

Song: _____

Source:_____ Date: _____

Genre/Mood: _____ Tempo:_____

Chords/Notes:_____

_____

_____

_____

Song: _____

Source:_____ Date: _____

Genre/Mood: _____ Tempo:_____

Chords/Notes:_____

_____

_____

_____

Song: _____

Source:_____ Date: _____

Genre/Mood: _____ Tempo:_____

Chords/Notes:_____

_____

_____

_____

Song: _____

Source:_____ Date: _____

Genre/Mood: _____ Tempo:_____

Chords/Notes:_____

_____

_____

_____

Song: _____

Source:_____ Date: _____

Genre/Mood: _____ Tempo:_____

Chords/Notes:_____

_____

_____

_____

N

Song: _____

Source:_____ Date: _____

Genre/Mood: _____ Tempo:_____

Chords/Notes:_____

_____

_____

_____

Song: _____

Source:_____ Date: _____

Genre/Mood: _____ Tempo:_____

Chords/Notes:_____

_____

_____

_____

Song: _____

Source:_____ Date: _____

Genre/Mood: _____ Tempo:_____

Chords/Notes:_____

_____

_____

_____

Song: _____

Source:_____ Date: _____

Genre/Mood: _____ Tempo:_____

Chords/Notes:_____

_____

_____

_____

Song: _____

Source:_____ Date: _____

Genre/Mood: _____ Tempo:_____

Chords/Notes:_____

_____

_____

_____

Song: _____

Source:_____ Date: _____

Genre/Mood: _____ Tempo:_____

Chords/Notes:_____

_____

_____

_____

N

Song: _____

Source:_____ Date: _____

Genre/Mood: _____ Tempo:_____

Chords/Notes:_____

_____

_____

_____

Song: _____

Source:_____ Date: _____

Genre/Mood: _____ Tempo:_____

Chords/Notes:_____

_____

_____

_____

Song: _____

Source:_____ Date: _____

Genre/Mood: _____ Tempo:_____

Chords/Notes:_____

_____

_____

_____

Song: _____

Source:_____ Date: _____

Genre/Mood: _____ Tempo:_____

Chords/Notes:_____

_____

_____

_____

Song: _____

Source:_____ Date: _____

Genre/Mood: _____ Tempo:_____

Chords/Notes:_____

_____

_____

_____

Song: _____

Source:_____ Date: _____

Genre/Mood: _____ Tempo:_____

Chords/Notes:_____

_____

_____

_____

N

Song: _____

Source:_____ Date: _____

Genre/Mood: _____ Tempo:_____

Chords/Notes:_____

_____

_____

_____

Song: _____

Source:_____ Date: _____

Genre/Mood: _____ Tempo:_____

Chords/Notes:_____

_____

_____

_____

Song: _____

Source:_____ Date: _____

Genre/Mood: _____ Tempo:_____

Chords/Notes:_____

_____

_____

_____

Song: _____

Source:_____ Date: _____

Genre/Mood: _____ Tempo:_____

Chords/Notes:_____

_____

_____

_____

0

Song: _____

Source:_____ Date: _____

Genre/Mood: _____ Tempo:_____

Chords/Notes:_____

_____

_____

_____

Song: _____

Source:_____ Date: _____

Genre/Mood: _____ Tempo:_____

Chords/Notes:_____

_____

_____

_____

Song: _____

Source:_____ Date: _____

Genre/Mood: _____ Tempo:_____

Chords/Notes:_____

_____

_____

_____

O

Song: _____

Source:_____ Date: _____

Genre/Mood: _____ Tempo:_____

Chords/Notes:_____

_____

_____

_____

Song: _____

Source:_____ Date: _____

Genre/Mood: _____ Tempo:_____

Chords/Notes:_____

_____

_____

_____

Song: _____

Source:_____ Date: _____

Genre/Mood: _____ Tempo:_____

Chords/Notes:_____

_____

_____

_____

0

Song: _____

Source:_____ Date: _____

Genre/Mood: _____ Tempo:_____

Chords/Notes:_____

_____

_____

_____

Song: _____

Source:_____ Date: _____

Genre/Mood: _____ Tempo:_____

Chords/Notes:_____

_____

_____

_____

Song: _____

Source:_____ Date: _____

Genre/Mood: _____ Tempo:_____

Chords/Notes:_____

_____

_____

_____

0

Song: _____

Source:_____ Date: _____

Genre/Mood: _____ Tempo:_____

Chords/Notes:_____

_____

_____

_____

Song: _____

Source:_____ Date: _____

Genre/Mood: _____ Tempo:_____

Chords/Notes:_____

_____

_____

_____

Song: _____

Source:_____ Date: _____

Genre/Mood: _____ Tempo:_____

Chords/Notes:_____

_____

_____

_____

0

Song: _____

Source:_____ Date: _____

Genre/Mood: _____ Tempo:_____

Chords/Notes:_____

_____

_____

_____

Song: _____

Source:_____ Date: _____

Genre/Mood: _____ Tempo:_____

Chords/Notes:_____

_____

_____

_____

Song: _____

Source:_____ Date: _____

Genre/Mood: _____ Tempo:_____

Chords/Notes:_____

_____

_____

_____

0

Song: _____

Source:_____ Date: _____

Genre/Mood: _____ Tempo:_____

Chords/Notes:_____

_____

_____

_____

Song: _____

Source:_____ Date: _____

Genre/Mood: _____ Tempo:_____

Chords/Notes:_____

_____

_____

_____

Song: _____

Source:_____ Date: _____

Genre/Mood: _____ Tempo:_____

Chords/Notes:_____

_____

_____

_____

Song: _____

Source:_____ Date: _____

Genre/Mood: _____ Tempo:_____

Chords/Notes:_____

_____

_____

_____

P

Song: _____

Source:_____ Date: _____

Genre/Mood: _____ Tempo:_____

Chords/Notes:_____

_____

_____

_____

Song: _____

Source:_____ Date: _____

Genre/Mood: _____ Tempo:_____

Chords/Notes:_____

_____

_____

_____

Song: _____

Source:_____ Date: _____

Genre/Mood: _____ Tempo:_____

Chords/Notes:_____

_____

_____

_____

P

Song: _____

Source:_____ Date: _____

Genre/Mood: _____ Tempo:_____

Chords/Notes:_____

_____

_____

_____

Song: _____

Source:_____ Date: _____

Genre/Mood: _____ Tempo:_____

Chords/Notes:_____

_____

_____

_____

Song: _____

Source:_____ Date: _____

Genre/Mood: _____ Tempo:_____

Chords/Notes:_____

_____

_____

_____

P

Song: _____

Source:_____ Date: _____

Genre/Mood: _____ Tempo:_____

Chords/Notes:_____

_____

_____

_____

Song: _____

Source:_____ Date: _____

Genre/Mood: _____ Tempo:_____

Chords/Notes:_____

_____

_____

_____

Song: _____

Source:_____ Date: _____

Genre/Mood: _____ Tempo:_____

Chords/Notes:_____

_____

_____

_____

P

Song: _____

Source:_____ Date: _____

Genre/Mood: _____ Tempo:_____

Chords/Notes:_____

_____

_____

_____

Song: _____

Source:_____ Date: _____

Genre/Mood: _____ Tempo:_____

Chords/Notes:_____

_____

_____

_____

Song: _____

Source:_____ Date: _____

Genre/Mood: _____ Tempo:_____

Chords/Notes:_____

_____

_____

_____

Song: _____

Source:_____ Date: _____

Genre/Mood: _____ Tempo:_____

Chords/Notes:_____

_____

_____

_____

Song: _____

Source:_____ Date: _____

Genre/Mood: _____ Tempo:_____

Chords/Notes:_____

_____

_____

_____

Song: _____

Source:_____ Date: _____

Genre/Mood: _____ Tempo:_____

Chords/Notes:_____

_____

_____

_____

P

Song: _____

Source:_____ Date: _____

Genre/Mood: _____ Tempo:_____

Chords/Notes:_____

_____

_____

_____

Song: _____

Source:_____ Date: _____

Genre/Mood: _____ Tempo:_____

Chords/Notes:_____

_____

_____

_____

Song: _____

Source:_____ Date: _____

Genre/Mood: _____ Tempo:_____

Chords/Notes:_____

_____

_____

_____

Q

Song: _____

Source:_____ Date: _____

Genre/Mood: _____ Tempo: _____

Chords/Notes: _____

_____

_____

_____

Song: _____

Source:_____ Date: _____

Genre/Mood: _____ Tempo:_____

Chords/Notes:_____

_____

_____

_____

Song: _____

Source:_____ Date: _____

Genre/Mood: _____ Tempo:_____

Chords/Notes:_____

_____

_____

_____

Song: _____

Source:_____ Date: _____

Genre/Mood: _____ Tempo:_____

Chords/Notes:_____

_____

_____

_____

Song: _____

Source:_____ Date: _____

Genre/Mood: _____ Tempo:_____

Chords/Notes:_____

_____

_____

_____

Song: _____

Source:_____ Date: _____

Genre/Mood: _____ Tempo:_____

Chords/Notes:_____

_____

_____

_____

Q

Song: _____

Source:_____ Date: _____

Genre/Mood: _____ Tempo: _____

Chords/Notes: _____

_____

_____

_____

Song: _____

Source:_____ Date: _____

Genre/Mood: _____ Tempo:_____

Chords/Notes:_____

_____

_____

_____

Song: _____

Source:_____ Date: _____

Genre/Mood: _____ Tempo:_____

Chords/Notes:_____

_____

_____

_____

Song: _____

Source:_____ Date: _____

Genre/Mood: _____ Tempo:_____

Chords/Notes:_____

_____

_____

_____

Song: _____

Source:_____ Date: _____

Genre/Mood: _____ Tempo:_____

Chords/Notes:_____

_____

_____

_____

Song: _____

Source:_____ Date: _____

Genre/Mood: _____ Tempo:_____

Chords/Notes:_____

_____

_____

_____

Q

Song: _____

Source: _____ Date: _____

Genre/Mood: _____ Tempo: _____

Chords/Notes: _____

_____

_____

_____

Song: _____

Source: _____ Date: _____

Genre/Mood: _____ Tempo: _____

Chords/Notes: _____

_____

_____

_____

Song: _____

Source: _____ Date: _____

Genre/Mood: _____ Tempo: _____

Chords/Notes: _____

_____

_____

_____

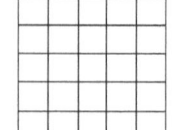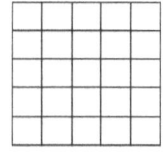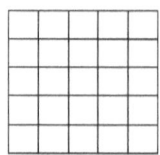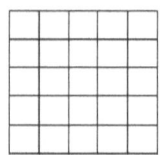

Song: _____

Source:_____ Date: _____

Genre/Mood: _____ Tempo:_____

Chords/Notes:_____

_____

_____

_____

Song: _____

Source:_____ Date: _____

Genre/Mood: _____ Tempo:_____

Chords/Notes:_____

_____

_____

_____

Song: _____

Source:_____ Date: _____

Genre/Mood: _____ Tempo:_____

Chords/Notes:_____

_____

_____

_____

Song: _____

Source:_____ Date: _____

Genre/Mood: _____ Tempo:_____

Chords/Notes:_____

_____

_____

_____

R

Song: _____

Source:_____ Date: _____

Genre/Mood: _____ Tempo:_____

Chords/Notes:_____

_____

_____

_____

Song: _____

Source:_____ Date: _____

Genre/Mood: _____ Tempo:_____

Chords/Notes:_____

_____

_____

_____

Song: _____

Source:_____ Date: _____

Genre/Mood: _____ Tempo:_____

Chords/Notes:_____

_____

_____

_____

Song: _____

Source:_____ Date: _____

Genre/Mood: _____ Tempo:_____

Chords/Notes:_____

_____

_____

_____

Song: _____

Source:_____ Date: _____

Genre/Mood: _____ Tempo:_____

Chords/Notes:_____

_____

_____

_____

Song: _____

Source:_____ Date: _____

Genre/Mood: _____ Tempo:_____

Chords/Notes:_____

_____

_____

_____

R

Song: _____

Source:_____ Date: _____

Genre/Mood: _____ Tempo:_____

Chords/Notes:_____

_____

_____

_____

Song: _____

Source:_____ Date: _____

Genre/Mood: _____ Tempo:_____

Chords/Notes:_____

_____

_____

_____

Song: _____

Source:_____ Date: _____

Genre/Mood: _____ Tempo:_____

Chords/Notes:_____

_____

_____

_____

Song: _____

Source:_____ Date: _____

Genre/Mood: _____ Tempo:_____

Chords/Notes:_____

_____

_____

_____

Song: _____

Source:_____ Date: _____

Genre/Mood: _____ Tempo:_____

Chords/Notes:_____

_____

_____

_____

Song: _____

Source:_____ Date: _____

Genre/Mood: _____ Tempo:_____

Chords/Notes:_____

_____

_____

_____

R

Song: _____

Source:_____ Date: _____

Genre/Mood: _____ Tempo:_____

Chords/Notes:_____

_____

_____

_____

Song: _____

Source:_____ Date: _____

Genre/Mood: _____ Tempo:_____

Chords/Notes:_____

_____

_____

_____

Song: _____

Source:_____ Date: _____

Genre/Mood: _____ Tempo:_____

Chords/Notes:_____

_____

_____

_____

Song: _____

Source:_____ Date: _____

Genre/Mood: _____ Tempo:_____

Chords/Notes:_____

_____

_____

_____

S

Song: _____

Source:_____ Date: _____

Genre/Mood: _____ Tempo:_____

Chords/Notes:_____

_____

_____

_____

Song: _____

Source:_____ Date: _____

Genre/Mood: _____ Tempo:_____

Chords/Notes:_____

_____

_____

_____

Song: _____

Source:_____ Date: _____

Genre/Mood: _____ Tempo:_____

Chords/Notes:_____

_____

_____

_____

S

Song: _____

Source:_____ Date: _____

Genre/Mood: _____ Tempo:_____

Chords/Notes:_____

_____

_____

_____

Song: _____

Source:_____ Date: _____

Genre/Mood: _____ Tempo:_____

Chords/Notes:_____

_____

_____

_____

Song: _____

Source:_____ Date: _____

Genre/Mood: _____ Tempo:_____

Chords/Notes:_____

_____

_____

_____

Song: _____

Source:_____ Date: _____

Genre/Mood: _____ Tempo:_____

Chords/Notes:_____

_____

_____

_____

Song: _____

Source:_____ Date: _____

Genre/Mood: _____ Tempo:_____

Chords/Notes:_____

_____

_____

_____

Song: _____

Source:_____ Date: _____

Genre/Mood: _____ Tempo:_____

Chords/Notes:_____

_____

_____

_____

S

Song: _____

Source:_____ Date: _____

Genre/Mood: _____ Tempo:_____

Chords/Notes:_____

_____

_____

_____

Song: _____

Source:_____ Date: _____

Genre/Mood: _____ Tempo:_____

Chords/Notes:_____

_____

_____

_____

Song: _____

Source:_____ Date: _____

Genre/Mood: _____ Tempo:_____

Chords/Notes:_____

_____

_____

_____

S

Song: _____

Source:_____ Date: _____

Genre/Mood: _____ Tempo:_____

Chords/Notes:_____

_____

_____

_____

Song: _____

Source:_____ Date: _____

Genre/Mood: _____ Tempo:_____

Chords/Notes:_____

_____

_____

_____

Song: _____

Source:_____ Date: _____

Genre/Mood: _____ Tempo:_____

Chords/Notes:_____

_____

_____

_____

S

Song: _____

Source:_____ Date: _____

Genre/Mood: _____ Tempo:_____

Chords/Notes:_____

_____

_____

_____

Song: _____

Source:_____ Date: _____

Genre/Mood: _____ Tempo:_____

Chords/Notes:_____

_____

_____

_____

Song: _____

Source:_____ Date: _____

Genre/Mood: _____ Tempo:_____

Chords/Notes:_____

_____

_____

_____

Song: _____

Source:_____ Date: _____

Genre/Mood: _____ Tempo:_____

Chords/Notes:_____

_____

_____

_____

T

Song: _____

Source:_____ Date: _____

Genre/Mood: _____ Tempo:_____

Chords/Notes:_____

_____

_____

_____

Song: _____

Source:_____ Date: _____

Genre/Mood: _____ Tempo:_____

Chords/Notes:_____

_____

_____

_____

Song: _____

Source:_____ Date: _____

Genre/Mood: _____ Tempo:_____

Chords/Notes:_____

_____

_____

_____

T

Song: _____

Source:_____ Date: _____

Genre/Mood: _____ Tempo:_____

Chords/Notes:_____

_____

_____

_____

Song: _____

Source:_____ Date: _____

Genre/Mood: _____ Tempo:_____

Chords/Notes:_____

_____

_____

_____

Song: _____

Source:_____ Date: _____

Genre/Mood: _____ Tempo:_____

Chords/Notes:_____

_____

_____

_____

T

Song: _____

Source:_____ Date: _____

Genre/Mood: _____ Tempo:_____

Chords/Notes:_____

_____

_____

_____

Song: _____

Source:_____ Date: _____

Genre/Mood: _____ Tempo:_____

Chords/Notes:_____

_____

_____

_____

Song: _____

Source:_____ Date: _____

Genre/Mood: _____ Tempo:_____

Chords/Notes:_____

_____

_____

_____

T

Song: _____

Source:_____ Date: _____

Genre/Mood: _____ Tempo:_____

Chords/Notes:_____

_____

_____

_____

Song: _____

Source:_____ Date: _____

Genre/Mood: _____ Tempo:_____

Chords/Notes:_____

_____

_____

_____

Song: _____

Source:_____ Date: _____

Genre/Mood: _____ Tempo:_____

Chords/Notes:_____

_____

_____

_____

T

Song: _____

Source:_____ Date: _____

Genre/Mood: _____ Tempo:_____

Chords/Notes:_____

_____

_____

_____

Song: _____

Source:_____ Date: _____

Genre/Mood: _____ Tempo:_____

Chords/Notes:_____

_____

_____

_____

Song: _____

Source:_____ Date: _____

Genre/Mood: _____ Tempo:_____

Chords/Notes:_____

_____

_____

_____

T

Song: _____

Source:_____ Date: _____

Genre/Mood: _____ Tempo:_____

Chords/Notes:_____

_____

_____

_____

Song: _____

Source:_____ Date: _____

Genre/Mood: _____ Tempo:_____

Chords/Notes:_____

_____

_____

_____

Song: _____

Source:_____ Date: _____

Genre/Mood: _____ Tempo:_____

Chords/Notes:_____

_____

_____

_____

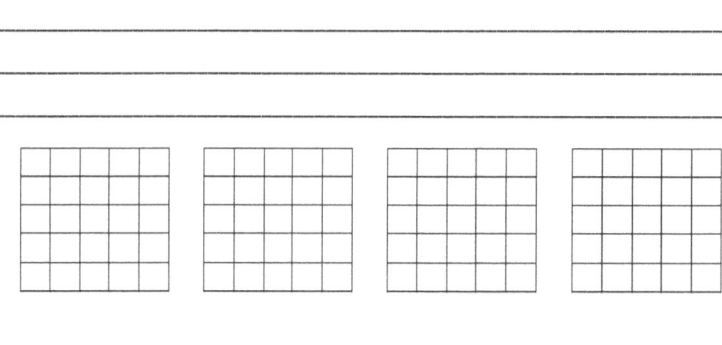

U

Song: _____

Source:_____ Date: _____

Genre/Mood: _____ Tempo: _____

Chords/Notes: _____

_____

_____

_____

Song: _____

Source:_____ Date: _____

Genre/Mood: _____ Tempo:_____

Chords/Notes:_____

_____

_____

_____

Song: _____

Source:_____ Date: _____

Genre/Mood: _____ Tempo:_____

Chords/Notes:_____

_____

_____

_____

Song: _____

Source:_____ Date: _____

Genre/Mood: _____ Tempo:_____

Chords/Notes:_____

_____

_____

_____

Song: _____

Source:_____ Date: _____

Genre/Mood: _____ Tempo:_____

Chords/Notes:_____

_____

_____

_____

Song: _____

Source:_____ Date: _____

Genre/Mood: _____ Tempo:_____

Chords/Notes:_____

_____

_____

_____

U

Song: _____

Source:_____ Date: _____

Genre/Mood: _____ Tempo: _____

Chords/Notes: _____

_____

_____

_____

Song: _____

Source:_____ Date: _____

Genre/Mood: _____ Tempo:_____

Chords/Notes:_____

_____

_____

_____

Song: _____

Source:_____ Date: _____

Genre/Mood: _____ Tempo:_____

Chords/Notes:_____

_____

_____

_____

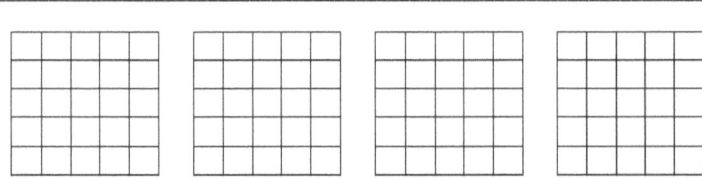

Song: _____

Source:_____ Date: _____

Genre/Mood: _____ Tempo:_____

Chords/Notes:_____

_____

_____

_____

Song: _____

Source:_____ Date: _____

Genre/Mood: _____ Tempo:_____

Chords/Notes:_____

_____

_____

_____

Song: _____

Source:_____ Date: _____

Genre/Mood: _____ Tempo:_____

Chords/Notes:_____

_____

_____

_____

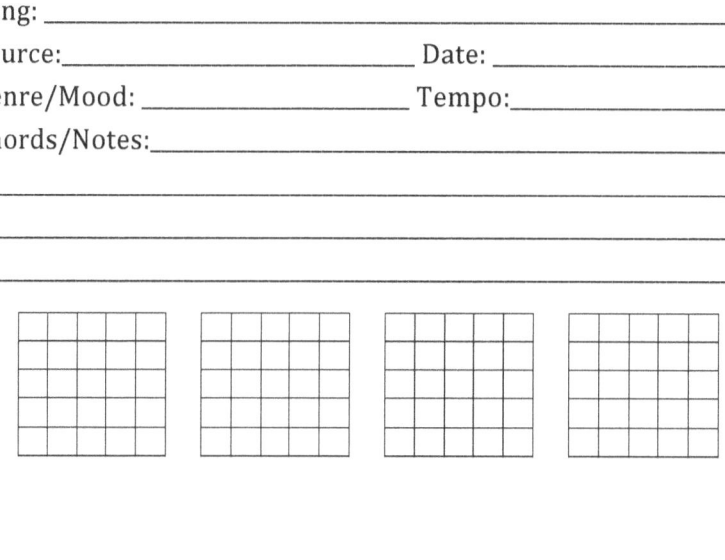

U

Song: _____

Source:_____ Date: _____

Genre/Mood: _____ Tempo: _____

Chords/Notes: _____

_____

_____

_____

Song: _____

Source:_____ Date: _____

Genre/Mood: _____ Tempo:_____

Chords/Notes:_____

_____

_____

_____

Song: _____

Source:_____ Date: _____

Genre/Mood: _____ Tempo:_____

Chords/Notes:_____

_____

_____

_____

Song: _____

Source:_____ Date: _____

Genre/Mood: _____ Tempo:_____

Chords/Notes:_____

_____

_____

_____

Song: _____

Source:_____ Date: _____

Genre/Mood: _____ Tempo:_____

Chords/Notes:_____

_____

_____

_____

Song: _____

Source:_____ Date: _____

Genre/Mood: _____ Tempo:_____

Chords/Notes:_____

_____

_____

_____

Song: _____

Source:_____ Date: _____

Genre/Mood: _____ Tempo:_____

Chords/Notes:_____

_____

_____

_____

V

Song: _____

Source:_____ Date: _____

Genre/Mood: _____ Tempo:_____

Chords/Notes:_____

_____

_____

_____

Song: _____

Source:_____ Date: _____

Genre/Mood: _____ Tempo:_____

Chords/Notes:_____

_____

_____

_____

Song: _____

Source:_____ Date: _____

Genre/Mood: _____ Tempo:_____

Chords/Notes:_____

_____

_____

_____

V

Song: _____

Source:_____ Date: _____

Genre/Mood: _____ Tempo:_____

Chords/Notes:_____

_____

_____

_____

Song: _____

Source:_____ Date: _____

Genre/Mood: _____ Tempo:_____

Chords/Notes:_____

_____

_____

_____

Song: _____

Source:_____ Date: _____

Genre/Mood: _____ Tempo:_____

Chords/Notes:_____

_____

_____

_____

V

Song: _____

Source:_____ Date: _____

Genre/Mood: _____ Tempo:_____

Chords/Notes:_____

_____

_____

_____

Song: _____

Source:_____ Date: _____

Genre/Mood: _____ Tempo:_____

Chords/Notes:_____

_____

_____

_____

Song: _____

Source:_____ Date: _____

Genre/Mood: _____ Tempo:_____

Chords/Notes:_____

_____

_____

_____

Song: _____

Source:_____ Date: _____

Genre/Mood: _____ Tempo:_____

Chords/Notes:_____

_____

_____

_____

Song: _____

Source:_____ Date: _____

Genre/Mood: _____ Tempo:_____

Chords/Notes:_____

_____

_____

_____

V

Song: _____

Source:_____ Date: _____

Genre/Mood: _____ Tempo:_____

Chords/Notes:_____

_____

_____

_____

V

Song: _____

Source:_____ Date: _____

Genre/Mood: _____ Tempo:_____

Chords/Notes:_____

_____

_____

_____

Song: _____

Source:_____ Date: _____

Genre/Mood: _____ Tempo:_____

Chords/Notes:_____

_____

_____

_____

Song: _____

Source:_____ Date: _____

Genre/Mood: _____ Tempo:_____

Chords/Notes:_____

_____

_____

_____

Song: _____

Source:_____ Date: _____

Genre/Mood: _____ Tempo:_____

Chords/Notes:_____

_____

_____

_____

Song: _____

Source:_____ Date: _____

Genre/Mood: _____ Tempo:_____

Chords/Notes:_____

_____

_____

_____

Song: _____

Source:_____ Date: _____

Genre/Mood: _____ Tempo:_____

Chords/Notes:_____

_____

_____

_____

Song: _____

Source:_____ Date: _____

Genre/Mood: _____ Tempo:_____

Chords/Notes:_____

_____

_____

_____

W

Song: _____

Source:_____ Date: _____

Genre/Mood: _____ Tempo:_____

Chords/Notes:_____

_____

_____

_____

Song: _____

Source:_____ Date: _____

Genre/Mood: _____ Tempo:_____

Chords/Notes:_____

_____

_____

_____

Song: _____

Source:_____ Date: _____

Genre/Mood: _____ Tempo:_____

Chords/Notes:_____

_____

_____

_____

W

Song: _____

Source:_____ Date: _____

Genre/Mood: _____ Tempo:_____

Chords/Notes:_____

_____

_____

_____

Song: _____

Source:_____ Date: _____

Genre/Mood: _____ Tempo:_____

Chords/Notes:_____

_____

_____

_____

Song: _____

Source:_____ Date: _____

Genre/Mood: _____ Tempo:_____

Chords/Notes:_____

_____

_____

_____

W

Song: _____

Source:_____ Date: _____

Genre/Mood: _____ Tempo:_____

Chords/Notes:_____

_____

_____

_____

Song: _____

Source:_____ Date: _____

Genre/Mood: _____ Tempo:_____

Chords/Notes:_____

_____

_____

_____

Song: _____

Source:_____ Date: _____

Genre/Mood: _____ Tempo:_____

Chords/Notes:_____

_____

_____

_____

Song: _____

Source:_____ Date: _____

Genre/Mood: _____ Tempo:_____

Chords/Notes:_____

_____

_____

_____

Song: _____
Source:_____ Date: _____
Genre/Mood: _____ Tempo:_____
Chords/Notes:_____
_____
_____
_____

Song: _____
Source:_____ Date: _____
Genre/Mood: _____ Tempo:_____
Chords/Notes:_____
_____
_____
_____

W

Song: _____
Source:_____ Date: _____
Genre/Mood: _____ Tempo:_____
Chords/Notes:_____
_____
_____
_____

Song: _____

Source:_____ Date: _____

Genre/Mood: _____ Tempo:_____

Chords/Notes:_____

_____

_____

_____

Song: _____

Source:_____ Date: _____

Genre/Mood: _____ Tempo:_____

Chords/Notes:_____

_____

_____

_____

Song: _____

Source:_____ Date: _____

Genre/Mood: _____ Tempo:_____

Chords/Notes:_____

_____

_____

_____

X

Song: _____

Source:_____ Date: _____

Genre/Mood: _____ Tempo:_____

Chords/Notes:_____

_____

_____

_____

Song: _____

Source:_____ Date: _____

Genre/Mood: _____ Tempo:_____

Chords/Notes:_____

_____

_____

_____

Song: _____

Source:_____ Date: _____

Genre/Mood: _____ Tempo:_____

Chords/Notes:_____

_____

_____

_____

X

Song: _____

Source:_____ Date: _____

Genre/Mood: _____ Tempo:_____

Chords/Notes:_____

_____

_____

_____

Song: _____

Source:_____ Date: _____

Genre/Mood: _____ Tempo:_____

Chords/Notes:_____

_____

_____

_____

Song: _____

Source:_____ Date: _____

Genre/Mood: _____ Tempo:_____

Chords/Notes:_____

_____

_____

_____

Y

Song: _____

Source:_____ Date: _____

Genre/Mood: _____ Tempo: _____

Chords/Notes: _____

_____

_____

_____

Song: _____

Source:_____ Date: _____

Genre/Mood: _____ Tempo:_____

Chords/Notes:_____

_____

_____

_____

Song: _____

Source:_____ Date: _____

Genre/Mood: _____ Tempo:_____

Chords/Notes:_____

_____

_____

_____

Song: _____

Source:_____ Date: _____

Genre/Mood: _____ Tempo:_____

Chords/Notes:_____

_____

_____

_____

Song: _____

Source:_____ Date: _____

Genre/Mood: _____ Tempo:_____

Chords/Notes:_____

_____

_____

_____

Song: _____

Source:_____ Date: _____

Genre/Mood: _____ Tempo:_____

Chords/Notes:_____

_____

_____

_____

Y

Song: _____

Source:_____ Date: _____

Genre/Mood: _____ Tempo: _____

Chords/Notes: _____

_____

_____

_____

Song: _____

Source:_____ Date: _____

Genre/Mood: _____ Tempo:_____

Chords/Notes:_____

_____

_____

_____

Song: _____

Source:_____ Date: _____

Genre/Mood: _____ Tempo:_____

Chords/Notes:_____

_____

_____

_____

Song: _____

Source:_____ Date: _____

Genre/Mood: _____ Tempo:_____

Chords/Notes:_____

_____

_____

_____

Song: _____

Source:_____ Date: _____

Genre/Mood: _____ Tempo:_____

Chords/Notes:_____

_____

_____

_____

Song: _____

Source:_____ Date: _____

Genre/Mood: _____ Tempo:_____

Chords/Notes:_____

_____

_____

_____

Y

Song: _____

Source: _____ Date: _____

Genre/Mood: _____ Tempo: _____

Chords/Notes: _____

_____

_____

_____

Song: _____

Source: _____ Date: _____

Genre/Mood: _____ Tempo: _____

Chords/Notes: _____

_____

_____

_____

Song: _____

Source: _____ Date: _____

Genre/Mood: _____ Tempo: _____

Chords/Notes: _____

_____

_____

_____

Song: _____
Source:_____ Date: _____
Genre/Mood: _____ Tempo:_____
Chords/Notes:_____
_____
_____
_____

Song: _____
Source:_____ Date: _____
Genre/Mood: _____ Tempo:_____
Chords/Notes:_____
_____
_____
_____

Song: _____
Source:_____ Date: _____
Genre/Mood: _____ Tempo:_____
Chords/Notes:_____
_____
_____
_____

Z

Song: _____

Source:_____ Date: _____

Genre/Mood: _____ Tempo:_____

Chords/Notes:_____

_____

_____

_____

Z

Song: _____

Source:_____ Date: _____

Genre/Mood: _____ Tempo:_____

Chords/Notes:_____

_____

_____

_____

Song: _____

Source:_____ Date: _____

Genre/Mood: _____ Tempo:_____

Chords/Notes:_____

_____

_____

_____

Song: _____

Source:_____ Date: _____

Genre/Mood: _____ Tempo:_____

Chords/Notes:_____

_____

_____

_____

Z

Song: _____

Source:_____ Date: _____

Genre/Mood: _____ Tempo:_____

Chords/Notes:_____

_____

_____

_____

Song: _____

Source:_____ Date: _____

Genre/Mood: _____ Tempo:_____

Chords/Notes:_____

_____

_____

_____

Song: _____

Source:_____ Date: _____

Genre/Mood: _____ Tempo:_____

Chords/Notes:_____

_____

_____

_____

Z

Song: _____

Source:_____ Date: _____

Genre/Mood: _____ Tempo:_____

Chords/Notes:_____

_____

_____

_____

Song: _____

Source:_____ Date: _____

Genre/Mood: _____ Tempo:_____

Chords/Notes:_____

_____

_____

_____

Song: _____

Source:_____ Date: _____

Genre/Mood: _____ Tempo:_____

Chords/Notes:_____

_____

_____

_____

Song: _____

Source:_____ Date: _____

Genre/Mood: _____ Tempo:_____

Chords/Notes:_____

_____

_____

_____

Song: _____

Source:_____ Date: _____

Genre/Mood: _____ Tempo:_____

Chords/Notes:_____

_____

_____

_____

Song: _____

Source:_____ Date: _____

Genre/Mood: _____ Tempo:_____

Chords/Notes:_____

_____

_____

_____

Z

Song: _____

Source:_____ Date: _____

Genre/Mood: _____ Tempo:_____

Chords/Notes:_____

_____

_____

_____

Song: _____

Source:_____ Date: _____

Genre/Mood: _____ Tempo:_____

Chords/Notes:_____

_____

_____

_____

Final Notes

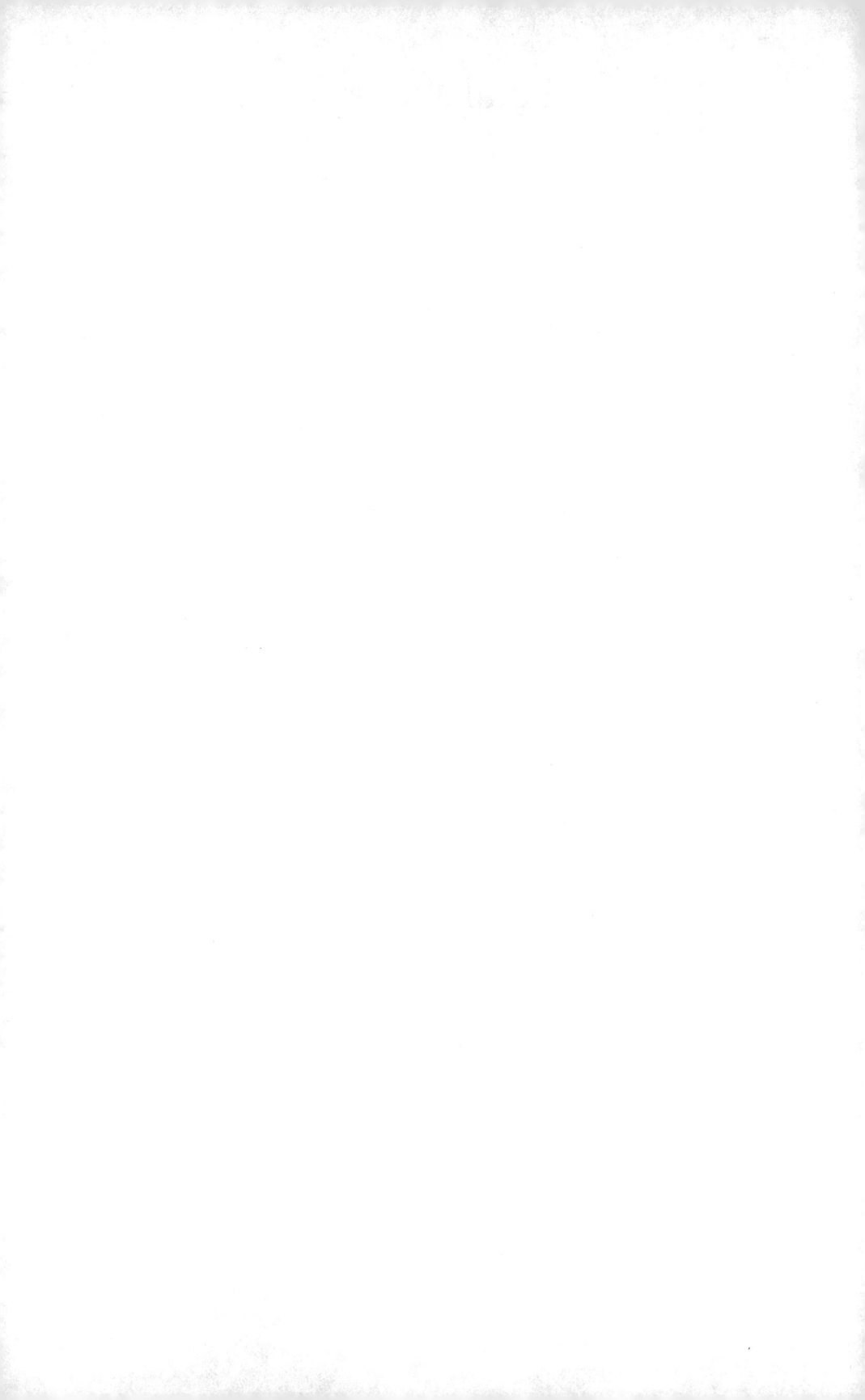

.